Photography
ZEN

By Roditch

Introduction

I am a photographer who owns a Canon G10 so I can concentrate on the image and not the equipment. There are four kinds of photography. I belong to the first kind which is art, or from the soul. This small book is about finding yourself, then finding out what yourself wants and cares about and then and only then does "making money" come into it or not. Two other kinds of photography belong to soulless and artless technical categories like: wedding photography and commercial photography. The fourth kind, is giving a shit photography which is often called photojournalism and sits equally with art when you are searching for the truth. These few pages can change your photography overnight. You need to understand that it is you, your soul, pressing the button and the images that come are pure reflections of your soul, every time.

Light

And then there was light, a natural light from the sun which is all you will ever need with some assistance from reflectors and tripods. Early morning light and evening light is perfect for most photos. In the middle of the day you need overcast lighting, never bright sun if you can help it. If you have to shoot people on a sunny day use a round ring with some kind of diffuser material in it, held over their heads. When shooting with natural light, a camera set on an ISO of 800 and has very low noise will be important. Also a tripod is very important and you should use one when you can, or something you can rest the camera on. I like light from all directions, it will depend on the situation whether you shoot with light on an angle of 45 degrees to your subject, in front, on the side or from behind. Most photography books will say the same thing, so it is important to adopt this into your photographic repertoire ASAP. I always use the M – Manual setting for exposures.

Where

Environment photography places emphasis on the place you take your photographs. The background is as important to your story as the subject and the foreground. Years ago I would put my camera on the tripod and move it around until I found a background that looked pretty good without a subject in it. Once found I would walk the subject onto "the stage" and think about how they would stand or sit. Often an old armchair, some steps, a doorway or window would look good. Then the foreground. They would often hold something in their hands, like a flower, a dog or a gun, depends on whose photo you are taking, and what is important for them, what they love and care about. Finally the expression which comes next.

Expression

  As with so many others Henri Cartier Bresson changed my photographic and personal life because he introduced me to the soul. The very entity that rides in our body through the world of joy and sorrow. Without expression from the soul there is no photograph, only ink lost on paper forever. Most famous painters know this and that's why their paintings are loved by so many and it was Henri Cartier Bresson who was able to capture in a moment what painters did in weeks. Expression is fleeting and often invisible so you have no hope of capturing it without capturing yourself first because if you don't your photos will be pretty meaningless. Expressions that are real and natural that reflect the true nature of a person are what I am talking about. Eyes, mouth, hands all tell a story, but you need to recognize the right moment and press the button quickly. I don't like a blank nothing, lifeless portraits as they don't tell you anything about the person apart from their taste in clothes.

Story

Every picture tells a story. Writing with light. Knowing more about you self and everyone you love is good for your soul. We nearly all keep our true selves hidden from the world, including ourselves, our friends and family. We are hiding our thoughts because they are full of doubt and confusion and secrets and we become ghosts in our culture and society. Photography can release the soul from its prison and let it out into the light of day and this has to be your sole purpose as a photographer. Everyone has a story worth telling, worth seeing and worth taking. Childhood, spirituality, work, sport, growing old, friends, family, politics, animals, the environment, suffering, homeless, schools, pollution, culture, race, farming, poverty, courage, beauty and nature. There are many stories you can tell and shed your light and insight with others. The story is what counts. Get a pencil and paper "right now" and write down one or two things or people you care about, draw pictures as you imagine you will take them, like a storyboard they use to make movies. Use the camera like you use your own eye, and record all the wonderful and not so wonderful things you see every day. Use your camera like your imagination and record what your imagination and your dreams see every day. Never forget photography means writing with light. As a photographer you are a light writer and a writer of light. And interestingly all spiritual traditions talk about light, and seeing the light, and enlightenment. As a photographer you have a spiritual connection with the world. You need to understand light and how it creates our reality, how it falls from the sky and without it, there is only darkness, a photograph of a black bird in the night. Everyday look at the light, how it falls on a flower, peeks through the clouds and lands on your dog's eyes. Sometimes it is gentle, warm, a soft yellow and others strong and hot. See how it floats down to the streets below and creates shadows that twist and turn with the people as they walk and run. Think how your life is changing as you become a light watcher and a light writer and how amazing everything is under the Sun.

What do I
do next?

One option is to take pictures of your favourite subject every day. A record of their time on earth. Capture the joy and sorrow, the events and places, the light and shade and after one or two years put the pictures into Microsoft Word and make a book. Print 10 copies and give them to the people who care and at the same time enjoy a fine wine and wonderful dinner, celebrate together. There is nothing more meaningful than the meaning happening before your eyes everyday as long as you have the heart to see it. This is not a book about "making money" Vincent Van Gogh never made a bean while he was alive and some, maybe most (including me) of the best photographers in the world have a second job, a second life, a second reason to live a rich and fulfilling life that gives you the perspective, the knowledge about life, the relationships with others that can never come as a "professional photographer" but can take you there. Make a plan to exhibit and publish your work and never look back. No matter how long it takes, you can love doing this.

Creativity

Children are good at it and we are scared of it. Just say it out aloud, I am scared of being creative. Children's minds up until the age of seven operate on the Alpha Mind Level which is the same as deep meditation. NASA has studied creativity and discovered it wanes around the same age, seven, when our minds become influenced by: society, parents, culture and schools and we operate on the Beta level, an over active mind. The only way to be one with your soul, create from your soul and be totally happy with your life is to function more on the Alpha level. This allows you to hear the birds singing, smell the flowers and use your intuition "the link from soul to conscious mind"

You can be more "Alpha" by spending more time with children and see how they function in the world, read children's books, meditate and just give up on being some kind of rich and serious person taking on the world. One option is to try the http://thesilvamethod.co.nz/the-alpha-dimension/.

Good Luck

You may be asking by now what has this to do with photography. When I was a Photography Teacher in College my main photography textbook was "As a man Thinketh by James Allen" because a photograph is all about you and how you think and see the world. Change your thoughts and change the world and change your photographs. It is up to you how far you go and how deep you go into yourself. I am sure Henri Cartier Bresson is one person who can help you understand the journey you can take into good photography. He is the master and he walked the talk. Never forget you live in a sea of digital cameras with trillions of images, yet Bresson used a 35mm Leica camera with film and no one will ever get past him.

About Me

I am over 60. My first camera was a Nikon F. I bought it when I was 17. I am a natural photographer (born with talent) and I was a Photography teacher for many years. I have been lost and found so many times trying to find my style, my voice, because I was never Alpha so my chattering mind led me down so many blind alleyways in such a (I am reflecting) stupid and unseeing way. But all's well that end's well. Now I now it is up to me what I photograph, how I photograph it and how I feel about it. The answer to good photography is absurdly simple, it is about your life and your journey, not money, so start sharing now.

A technical recap

No amount of technical skill makes a good photo, by itself.

Early morning, late evening and cloudy light is the best light for people pictures.

A fast shutter speed always helps, so buy a camera that shoots without noise at 800 ISO.

Shooting people inside, beside open doorways and windows gives great light, especially 45 degrees side on, Rembrandt lighting. A piece of white foam board is a great reflector to put more light into dark shadows.

Compose your photos of people with a plain background, like a single colour on a wall, and remember the three levels. Background, subject and foreground (what they are holding) are all important.

Expression is everything, without it the photo is lifeless. Light makes the expression on landscapes and helps make it on people.

Emotions; are people happy, sad, joyful? Capture it all.

If you need to take pictures of people in the midday sun, hold a 1 meter round sheet of muslin over their heads, to diffuse the light.

Colour helps make colour photographs more interesting, don't be scared to use lots of colour especially on cloudy days.

A tripod can help you take your time to make a picture, like the Mona Lisa. Don't worry when taking a picture, relax, and follow your instincts.

With portraits decide if you want to be close up, like head and shoulders, full length or environmental. If they have beautiful eyes then I will take a portrait very close. If they have interesting hands then I will do a ¾ shot. If their clothes are special then full length is good, either sitting or standing. If they like painting graffiti then an environmental photograph against their art will be good.

The photograph will last for centuries. Always remember how special every photograph you take of someone is, especially ones that capture them in a meaningful way. They will be a treasure forever.

The difference between a snap and a "professional photograph" is usually the intent of the photographer: how he/ she sees the world and how he/ she can capture what he/ she feels, very well and how he/ she uses light, composition, texture, contrast, expression, clarity, backgrounds and foregrounds. Often a snap is better than a highly technical picture without "feeling" and may benefit technically with some photoshop work.

Photoshop cannot make a bad picture good. When I was young I had a darkroom and processed all my black and white films and prints. A master at this was Ansel Adams who invented the Zone System which is an incredible way to take perfect photographs. The standard procedure in the darkroom was to choose the contrast of the paper you needed: 1 – 5 from no contrast to very contrasty. To expose the print and dodge the areas that were too dark by cupping your hands and blocking the light from the enlarger and burning in the areas that were too light by adding extra light to the print through a small hole in your hands that the light can pass through. I use photoshop for doing the same things as I did back then, burning, dodging, contrast. This can be a lot of fun when you get good at adding and reducing light on your photograph. The settings on these tools start at around 10%. Choose whether it is shadow, medium or highlights. Overuse of photoshop is a big mistake as it can never ever fix a bad photograph only enhance a good one.

Creativity is freedom. In a world where we conform to everything, the opportunity to say and feel what we really want is frightening for most people. So, let yourself go, believe in yourself, tell your stories, express yourself into the world, help others to see and understand, never ever say you can't do it, of course you can. Just start and tell your story and other people's stories. Write yourself with light into the world and other people's hearts, don't be afraid, don't be too technical, follow simple rules and either make a book or have an exhibition no matter how small every year. Creativity is all about you and your life and that's important isn't it.

Photographers I like

Henri Cartier Bresson
David Alan Harvey
Ansel Adams
Alfred Eisenstaedt
Dorothea Lange
Robert Maplethorpe
Yousuf Karsh

Cameras

Any camera that has very low noise at 1000 ISO

Sony-A9

Pentax-K1

Canon EOS 5d Mark IV

Nikon D600

Nikon D800

Nikon D7500

Nikon D5500

Sony A6300

Nikon D7200

Olympus OM-D E-M1 Mark II

Books

Any book by Thich Nhat Hanh
National Geographic Magazines
Robert Maplethorpe
The Bible – it is often about light
Any book on Buddhism
Any book by Alan Watts
Any book about Alpha Mind Level
Any book about Henri Cartier Bresson
Any classical painting portraiture books
Any classical painting books
Any book by Roditch
Any book by Ted Kooser – Poet
Any great poetry book

Life

The world is in trouble. The environment is getting worse with plastic in the oceans and radioactivity from Japan.

Governments are becoming more and more under the control of the Global Elite.

Internet censorship is ruining the internet for everyone.

Robots are coming and they will destroy our way of life. In many ways they already have by the computer code in our TV's phones and computers.

Social networks make us more and more crazy and dependent on technology.

5G technology is extremely dangerous for our health and it will destroy millions of lives.

Prosperity consciousness is misguided, false and dangerous.

Our dependence on technology and electricity is becoming more frightening the younger we are.

The lack of truth surrounding the origins of the bible creates an unreal world. Origins in Egypt, Buddhism and since the beginning of time.

Women are more intelligent and loving than men. It is important that women stop wanting to be men and focus on their powers of mind, intuition and love and take back their power.

The wrong thinking about living your life through a phone screen. The entertainment is a huge distraction from what is going on in the real world.

We think we are oh so smart with our ADOBE software and computer skills BUT not as smart as Plato, Socrates, William Butler Yeats, Jack London and the hundreds of writers, monks, artists and philosophers that created this civilization we are wrecking.

Happiness as a photographer comes from communing with your soul, creating meaning and helping the world and others.

Humility is something I have learnt these past 10 years. I am a willing worker for Jung's collective unconscious and I know so deep in my heart that the simple things in life matter and are our greatest challenges, like being happy, honest, prudent, wise, humble, healthy, mindful, helpful and kind. I am happy to be a drop in the ocean and feel the peace of knowing that I am part of the Earth, the Universe, the collective of all souls and all living things. Like a tree and a butterfly I am part of all life.

Thank you

Many thanks for buying this small book. I hope it's a life changer and you are happy. The book is small so you can get on with your great photography ASAP with insight and meaning.

Roditch 2019

www.ingramcontent.com/pod-product-compliance
Lightning Source LLC
Chambersburg PA
CBHW031942170526
45157CB00008B/3279